The Rule of Participation

Collected poems

Joyce James

© Joyce James 2017

All rights reserved. No part of this book may be reproduced or transmitted in any form or by any means, electronic or mechanical, or by any information or storage and retrieval system without permission in writing from the author or publisher.

Published by Compass Flower Press

an imprint of AKA-Publishing
Columbia, Missouri USA
www.AKA-Publishing.com

The Rule of Participation: Collected poems
Joyce James
ISBN: 978-1-942168-77-5

In honor of my parents,
    James Richard Osburn 1912–1987
    Mary Lou Noe Osburn, 1913–1987

my sisters,
    Barbara Jean Osburn 1949–1953
    Judith Ann Osburn Combs, 1943–1981
my brother,
    Donald Dean Osburn 1936–2016

my grandparents,
    Cora Mae Lee Noe and James Paul Noe
    Hiram Cooper Osburn and Allie Verona Curry Osburn

Thanks to the following literary journals and books where named poems first appeared:

The Missouri Review: "The Rule of Participation of Loving My Sister" (now entitled "The Rule of Participation")

Tendril Fifth Anniversary Issue: "In the Summer," "Mathematics" (now entitled "Her Photograph")

***Ploughshares, Special Poetry Issue* edited by Seamus Heaney**: "Catbirds," "Wild Canaries on a Twenty Mile Stretch of Highway"

Crazyhorse: "Their Anniversary," "Planting Trees in a Field My Father Dug the Rock From With his own Hands"

Ploughshares: "Dusk" (now entitled "Gypsy Territory")

The Ohio Review: "There Are the Lilacs"

Commonweal: "Raising Animals," "Playing Pizzicato"

The Southern Poetry Review: "Mrs. Stewart's Concentrated Bluing"

Gulf Coast: "Every Saturday Night," "Suffolk Ewes"

Shenandoah: "What the Bell Told"

The Louisville Review: "In Absentia"

The Gettysburg Review: "Never Dreaming He'd Have Two Daughters Die before Him"

The Southern Review: "Lies" (now entitled "Surveillance")

Cimarron Review: "Mid–July," "Burr Oak Church Community"

Eleven of these poems have appeared in *The Wild Canaries*, a chapbook published by Wings Press, 1992.

"The Wild Canaries on a Twenty–Mile Stretch of Highway" was reprinted in *The Anthology of Magazine Verse and Yearbook of American Poetry*, 1985.

A section of "The Lace School" appeared as "Belgium Wedding Lace" in *The Denny Poems*, 1987.

"Suffolk Ewes," "The Wild Canaries on a Twenty–Mile Stretch of Highway," "Raising Animals: After an Eve," and "Dusk" (now entitled "Gypsy Territory") were reprinted in *Inheritance of Light*, University of North Texas Press, 1996.

Contents

Wild Canaries on a Twenty-Mile Stretch of Highway 1
Nebraska Methodist Hospital 2
Her Photograph 3
Vigilance In Nodaway County 4
Never Dreaming He'd Have Two Daughters Die Before Him 5
The Bridge Over the Creek 6
Rainbow Dishes 7
She's Only Dreaming 8
Intuition 10
Paying Respects 13
Mid-July 14
Red Emperor Tulips 18
In Absentia 19
Their Anniversary 21
Tumultuous Weather 23
We Took the Flowers to Father 24
The Bath 25
High School Sweethearts 26
Playing Pizzicato 27
Mrs. Stewart's Concentrated Liquid Bluing 29
My Father's Cows 30
The Journey 31
Fairfax Community Hospital 32
The American Character 33
Frank Field's Weather Report 34
Memory's Fragment 35
Every Saturday Night 36
Jubilant 37
Grocery Shopping 38
Wolf School 40
Raising Animals 41
On Christmas Day, 1989 43
Yellow Short Haired Tabby 44
Driver's Ed 45
You Leave for the Office 46
The Day of the Trucks 47
Summer Journaling 48
Red Gloves 49
What the Bell Told 50

Threshing	51
Determined to Go Fishing	52
When School Is Out	53
Traveling North to Köln	54
Residing Next Door	55
Deer Season	56
Squatters	57
Burned to the Ground	58
Conversion at the Dome	59
The Rule of Participation	60
Ominous	61
Story Line	62
My Husband	63
The Lace School	64
Surveillance	65
Lies	66
There Are the Lilacs	67
Planting Trees in A Field My Father Dug Rocks From With His Own Hands	69
Eye Lashes That Blinked You Love Me	71
Gypsy Territory	72
The Autumn Moon	73
Black and White Snapshot	75
Visiting the Dickinson Homestead	76
Suffolk Ewes	78
Catbirds	79
Thank You	*83*
About the Poet	*85*
Honors	*87*

It is your voice
saying, for example, the word barn
that the writer wrote
but the barn you say
is a barn you know or knew. The voice
in your head, speaking as you read,
never says anything neutrally—
. . . .
And barn is only a noun—no verb
or subject has entered into sentence yet!
The voice you hear when you read to yourself
Is the clearest voice: you speak it
speaking to you.

    –Thomas Lux
    "The Voice You Hear When You Read Silently"

Wild Canaries on a Twenty-Mile Stretch of Highway

In a few days I identify them —
The bright-colored males floating and dipping
Toward the silver-green hedge rows
Where their nests teeter.

Bright yellow with black feathers fastened
To bodies, they fly up to elms, then down
Through batiste clouds,
Precious stones set in a blue-fabric sky.

I drive among them
Day after day caring for my sister
While they feed their young.
A highway winds and knots, solitary in each of us.

When she dies, I pick marigolds and search
For the dark mums
That she loved from my parents' garden,
Arranging them in two hand-woven baskets

I bought for her in Texas —
The others in a piece of her crockery collection.
For days I come back
Along this road to care for her children,

Her house, to brake and swerve.
I cannot reason with
The wire-haired possum
That knots belly-up on the traffic's white-line,

Dead in a position of ecstasy.
That's what it's like to be dead,
To be centered and sure
And never squinting or fearing the cock-eyed

Headlights of a slow, on-coming car,
While the living, night and day,
Hurry along the roads
And ditches taking care of each other.

Nebraska Methodist Hospital

The war is inside my head.
Last night, television with genocide.
My sister's hair is
Shorn after chemotherapy.
She looks like the actresses
In concentration camps.
After surgery, I go
To see her every four hours.
In the intensive care waiting room, we wait,
The magazines neatly folded, unread.
Her eyes are alert over the oxygen mask
And she raises only her index finger
To let me know she's there.
At noon, relatives waiting
Can walk a close corridor
To the wing of private wars.
She can't talk.
The method actors seemed frightened on TV,
They had shaved their heads,
The acting almost artless.

Her Photograph

The woven baskets I filled with marigolds
are stacked under the stairwell, empty.

Her eyeglasses for seeing in the distance
in a button tin or old envelope.

All were perfunctory gifts, sisterly.
In a drawer, the Bible has her favorite verses

marked, then copied with an upward slant,
looping higher and higher each line.

I searched for a notebook with any directive
she'd left me. I need to count her years over and over.

At times I hear her speaking to my silence.
Grieving breaks our hearts like storms breaks

the branches of trees splintering them into pieces.
Sometimes I hear the soft blood rushing in her veins.

We learned to cradle the moment and bargain
for death to have reason

but I'm without power to say goodbye.
I wait for her to rise up to Heaven like steam

from a frozen lake. I have only a single
unfaded photograph of her and a letter written

with care when first she was sick.
The letter, a year old, is about her children.

I like the photograph when she's three,
not smiling, formidable, sitting in a child's chair.

Vigilance In Nodaway County

I don't know, Mr. Lawyer. I don't know
about the shooting. I don't live here anymore.
I'm visiting my parents. I can't answer that.
I don't know if he tormented the grocer.
Clearing the table, Mother asks about subpoenas.
My father knows laws won't stop a bully
but no inkling a man will be gunned down soon.
What's with the clerk cussing out a young girl
for stealing a candy bar. Tempers flared!

Why didn't small town logic work this time.
Summer nights in our quaint village,
a frenzy of moths circle a lighted Budweiser sign.
In daylight, Nodaway County's sheriff meets
the farmers, the town depends on him,
he's a strong decent man. He advises to stand
together against the bully. Confronting him
in the pool hall, most of these men have
never held a pool cue—their expertise
straight rows, keeping spinning planters level.

Gambling for a good rain, some sun,
and a break in the weather is their game.

On the tractor seat, custodian of the land,
a farmer moves with circumspect
over grassy slopes, his schemata of land, his ideal.
Native grasses tell him that earth's wide rim
lies ahead, hang on tight, plant a straight line
even if it curves on the hill. Come on, orange tractor,
John Deere disc, McCormick planter.

The bully brags he's stolen hogs east of town,
except that family doesn't raise hogs.
He pockets a pack of Dentyne, flashing
a roll of hundred dollar bills as he leaves.
After the shot, his blonde wife tumbles out
the pickup to the ground, his heavy head's
against the horn. Standing in the intersection
my father sees white gunfire and steps back,

the noise was as deafening as the honking of winter geese,
flying in formation. Someone bundles the woman
into his arms, carries her away from the scene.
The shooter or shooters, who knows, may be a neighbor.

It's July. A sheep dog crouches, frightened
in a culvert. The FBI, the *New York Times*,
Chicago Tribune, St. Joseph News-Press, NBC, CNN,
and ABC televisions, neighboring sheriffs,
constables, all walk our narrow sidewalks
that lead to Skidmore High School, beauty shops,
and the drugstore. They go to the Pool Hall.
No one answers the questions.

In sunlight, the hedgerow's fruit, an eerie green,
the men at the filling station say hot, humid weather
grows bumper crops. My sister rouges her cheeks,
keeps a notebook. Her last day on earth,
she celebrates her small son's baseball victory.
They play catch across her bed. Accidentally, he throws
the ball like a bullet. He's her star hitter, her star pitcher.

Never Dreaming He'd Have Two Daughters Die Before Him

My father in his heavy denim jacket,
The front fastened against the weather
By copper buttons I thought were foreign coins,
Picks up a dead pig from the sow's first litter
And throws it on top of a shed.

I didn't understand that a crazed sow
Would eat her dead ones,
Or that sometimes a gilt will devour her young
When she tastes the afterbirth.
A farmer could lose a litter of newborns

As if the earth had sprung open.
Who knows what I thought
As he grabbed the spotted pig away.
What he told me was how in high school
he practiced on the sodded court

Until his shot perfect,
His tournament skill as exact as morning light.
The trophy is on our dining room buffet.
My sister saved it for him
From the closing of Daleview High,

And for herself the fixtures,
Replacing the acetylene lamps
That once had been there. Like the dead,
The school's white globes are beautiful and luminous,
Burning in her own living room.

I hated my father for leaving the pig there,
The hedge trees filtering the light
Into abstract patterns.
So I imagined its eyes, alive in sunshine
And the hooves moving up shingles.

The Bridge Over the Creek

Was one car at a time, the noisy planks
Announcing arrivals. A warm spring,
We leaned through the bridge's ironwork
Watching fox cubs pawing each other
In a jungle of grasses.
We couldn't hold back our laughter.
My sister loved animals:
Their dog, beautiful black fur in full regalia
Standing on the roof of her Plymouth,
The cat Jenny Lauper living up to the name.
Early this morning she left me,
Her roses by the front porch in full bloom.
The cubs, they've gone downstream.

Rainbow Dishes

A ritual after dinner on Sunday
my sister and I took
Mother's dishes
to the window
where light made it shimmer.
The blue swan, our favorite,
brought from Tennessee
by our grandmother.
I'm home to to be with my sister.

In the dim afternoon, Mother cradles
her face in her hands.
My father smokes his Camels,
stubbing them out one by one.
Their silence in every room.

She's Only Dreaming

it's ironic her young son
gathers natural minutiae,
sea shells and rocks as she did.
they both saved Pepsi bottle tops
in their desk drawer for some prize.
when she wakes she'll light the lamp,
dust the books on his shelf,
smaller books lower,
encyclopedias eye-level.
then holding hands,
they'll search the walnut grove,
for a sapling to grow tall,
his first son's a chair.

Intuition

Her children stare into space.
They want to know where the dead go.
Is it past their school, their hometown?
Can you drive there?
On a holiday, the boats drift by,
One has her name.
The answers to the questions
Hide under a sandy shelf,
Below the water's clean surface,
Under the river's current
Where Death is playing his song.

Burr Oak Church Community

This could be anyplace
Once I let go of the rope
Holding the man easing out
Onto the ice bringing back
The foolish calf.

He's not our father
Whose steps shuffle
Instead of the fast breaks he made
Down the basketball court
To the score in high school.

This is not the rock
Bigger than a cow
Where we sat and dug
Deceptive pockets and partitions
Into the ground.

Across the gully
Prairie trees are bare
In the winter, just
The imported evergreens beside
The house stay crisp

In the cold snows.
This could be
Anybody's house and not ours,
Someone else's neighbors and their sons
Driving by.

This could be the empty house
Of a farmer and his wife
Retired and moved to town.
No, I've got you —
I'll hold you.

Only young cattle
Will wander out on the unsure
Ice chancing a death

Of pneumonia and fever
In a wind chill that sinks

Far below zero.
Look, I've saved them all—
I've held onto the rope—
Even the ones
You won't recognize.

Paying Respects

The spring's sprouting seed planted
By the neighbors races toward the fencerows.

Yesterday she died. Today friends and relatives
Come bringing food, asking what they can do.

I motion to the door but my father turns away.
It's one of your cousins I tell him.

I know the traffic down the long hill will stop.
Are the loose planks crossing the river bridge

Knelling her finality? Our grief doesn't waver;
My father will suffer and move slower

While dealing with floods and droughts,
Even forgetting her. Whoever grieves into eternity?

The dry summer winds turn to cold winter.
No need staring patiently outside, nothing can change.

She was joyous, always smiling, happy in life.
The hum of traffic has left, it's gone

I dread tomorrow and the day after.

Mid-July

When I touch her hand
It is hers
And someone else's.

At Schooler's Funeral Home
Cool plaster
Safeholds the smile,

Havens the light
Under the lid.
If I dared to sit

Her up however stiffly
The word, the idea
Of handclasp would come back.

Still, she sleeps
Like a piece
Of fine porcelain

Displayed in a shop window
On a God-forsaken street.

I have failed.
I will fail again
Thinking of objects,

Knowing a world
That is either right or wrong.

When I wanted to see her yesterday
An undertaker was convincing.

It would be better to wait—
Tomorrow.

I thought that I should give her something—
A fortune cookie with a blessing inside
A note from here to there.

Here he comes,
A small dark man unpresuming
Born without clothes.

He is asking me to go home—
Everyone's waiting for you
To make the arrangements.

What about her!
What about her?

Instead I will push
A stubborn doll
All over town

And twist
Her arms in their sockets—
I am the mad child

Twisting the glass arms
So the lined palms
Can be read.

A cat with her kittens resting
Heavy-eyed on the steps
When my grandfather died,

My grandmother saying
She would never have
Three generations dressing
And powdering her in solicitous tones.

Now my sister
The gracious, quiet
Full-breasted puppet

With her voice
Cut out in the back
By his incision.

All ceremony
Seems like a wound
Inside her still bones.

We do not know so much—
Is geography inches or feet deep?
Where in Tennessee
Did our great-grandmother spin on the wheel?

Intricately weaving each lap robe,
Pedaling into the night.
Now a figure looming above
The sour lamplight.

When will I touch
My sister's hand again?

And how will I know
If it is hers or someone else's?

But the world is not real
Or imaginary.

The rest of them try to forget.
They keep busy—

As though it were
Something involuntary
Like dying.

It is true—
One month
Before she died
She was planning

To wear
The tissue-silk red
Dress with polka dots.

I believe last times belong to gloss—
To resolution, to criminal law.

She will turn to me—
A grown sister coming back to dance in mourning.
She will hold her emeralded hand
For me to admire.

Let others talk of time's mercy
She'll have nothing but loss and its quarrel.

What if the imaginary life
Rivals memory?

Where are those who held her hand,
Told her Jesus loves us and gives us everlasting life.

I see them behind the stove
While it's the two of us who will sway together,

Who will lie on the same part of a hill,
Saying rites, head to toe,

Head to toe
Hearing the mothering silences.

Red Emperor Tulips

After a leveling fire,
the church stand-in, a grove
of burr oaks. Gray ashes mixed
with glass shards mark
the missing-tooth square
where our place of worship had stood.

Past the foundation that was left
to her burial beside our baby Jeanne,
family and friends have heads bowed,
some clad in somber shades
of the melted stained glass.
They listen to the minister
pray about nothing we want to hear.

In a Polaroid print she sent,
she's sitting on the back steps,
smiling, her dark hair fades
into the background, her arms
circle her glorious red tulips.

Perhaps to recollect by definition
means memory's awful grammar—
I am forgetting, I am forgotten.

In Absentia

With them, the mornings were like church,
hushed and dark.
The ceremony of creaking
utensils made the first day-sounds,

cups of coffee rattling like heartbeats.
A slight whisper
of vowels and sworn words,
I stayed covered

by quilts with scalloped edges,
under patterns
more intricate than grammar,
double Wedding Ring, Dresden Plate,

pieces cut from outgrown dresses—
A poached egg symmetrically golden
like the winter sun,
Mother calling "Come down."

I saw him going toward the barn,
cold sludge underfoot,
leaning into a mizzle of sleet
in Key overalls

and his heavy denim coat,
burnished buttons down its front
like medals
for the way he went alone into the lots.

About good and evil,
work was right,
he said, fair and appropriate, the reason
they slept soundly, rising to plan a righteous day.

My father died at daybreak, breakfast time,
the smell of coffee through the corridor,
a good time for talking.
He supposed they would breakfast together

as they always had,
his hospital gown neat at the nape of his neck,
the strings tied and his back straight,
his relentless eyes shining out the same

as when he went,
head lowered against a determined wind
to make a living, work the stock,
the slow, steamy hogs and cattle,

the jivey newborns,
their maroon hides still wet.
All his mornings were technicolored,
gold sun, red barn,

Blue rain, green trees.
Resolute, he started the stubborn orange tractor
in freezing weather,
filling the air

with a clacking,
an indecipherable and loud gospel,
so that even now, I can close my eyes and hear
the rough-putt of engine, realizing

what stands between me and stark mornings is his industry.

Their Anniversary

Up there's the rooster who's no joke—
copper inside out, a craftsman cut the mould.

Top of the garage, he points the days drift
with bright abandon, a silent prognosticator

at rapt attention, an ideal place for broadcasting
all prevailing breezes and moving air currents.

The gift's from me to my parents—a weathervane—
for their fifty years in the same house

talking, although more to themselves—
an unwillingness to blame the other

for any misfortune, the tractor hard to start,
rough roads, the time gone too soon.

In the summer Mother tied their dog
so he could crawl under the smokehouse for shade.

My father on his hands and knees pleaded
to the animal he thought caught underneath to come.

The pet eyed him from the grassy mound over
our root cellar. Catching sight of the dog didn't

change his mood, he was deep into disaster.
My sister tells the story better than I do.

Putting a cold, shiny rooster up on the garage roof
quietly cock-a-doodle-doing

for their neighborhood is a gift given by grown children
since we still cause our parents grief.

How could I know he'd try to take grain to the roof?
It was the same, the evening he coaxed a starving,

wild kitten from a hole in the haymow.
His chambray-blue shirttails blowing in the night air,

his jockey shorts loose on his skinny legs,
Mother behind him—everyone who could help them, dead—

She's handing him what he calls out for—
a ladder, his gloves, the saw.

Tumultuous Weather

Driving in road gear
across the field, my father throws
the tractor into neutral,
lets it roll to a stop
against a wooden gate,
his dark hair blowing
in the strong wind.
Jumping over the fence,
he runs through the pasture,
no time to waste,
funnel clouds mean tornadoes.
At the door, we're huddled together,
waiting to take cover.

We Took the Flowers to Father

In the nursing home, he's on his side.
I bring the flowers from her funeral.
My father's asleep under a blanket.
Now he's alone.
I want to take him home. I promise another time.
He motions me away, waving to leave.
My strong father, covered in flannel.

The Bath

At home, I bathe
my father, the water
pours like small rivers
over his body,
his skin seems
candlelit within.
His shoulders strong
and impervious
even though his world's
almost gone,
like over-exposed photographs
where you can't make out the people.
I move the cloth
across his stomach
as flat as yours,
young grandson's.
He looks as if he's
making a decision.
I rub oil on his scalp and feet,
part and comb his hair
white as bleached linen.

High School Sweethearts

Asleep in his recliner, his hand in hers,
she says his hands are like his mother's.
His agile fingers moved
on real mother-of-pearl saxophone keys
playing for us. She read us books
while he perused magazine articles
of new farming practices.
He asks what she thinks of alternating grains
with legumes, the cash flow less
after soil testing, building a pond, a hedge
of multiflora roses for wildlife.
I take highway 71 North
through St. Joe when I visit them,
the closer I get, the sweeter the clovers.

Playing Pizzicato

Though my father carried a leather wallet
With folded blank checks,
My mother would snap shut, with a kissing sound,
Her coin purse, its gullet-pouch wadded full of dollar bills.
I can see her non-committal nodding
As Mrs. Fullerton dangled each priced item
Before our eyes like perfect-attendance badges.
She drove in, in a sputtering old model car
With a running board,
Stopped then shifted to neutral.

She carried a stiff cowhide bag stuffed
With samples of Watkins Products.
Piece after piece, she showed my mother
Every bottle, cake and tube in the black satchel,
Its alligator mouth ajar —
The pineapple-orange flavoring,
Oxblood shoe polish, allspice.
She plucked boxes from their elastic loops
Like a trained violinist playing pizzicato.

Then from even deeper, she'd pull
Spearmint toothpaste, coconut pudding mix,
Gelatin powder, tweezers,
A paperback book of four O. Henry stories
And baking powder.
The times my mother bought nothing
I was embarrassed.
Everything went back slowly into place
While we stared at the woman's feet, one leg
Four inches shorter than the other leg and laced
Into a platform-soled shoe.
I longed for the burn salve as she slid it away,
The top of its round-can pictured
A St. Bernard pulling his young mistress
Onto rocks, saving her from drowning.
I almost danced to smell the apple-blossom talc
She pronounced with a big flourish,

Her dentures loose on the last word.
After she left I heard my mother tell
My father she always arrives right at dinnertime
When the table's already been set.

Mrs. Stewart's Concentrated Liquid Bluing

I think of the sheets dropped from the clothesline
on winter washday mornings like messages,
pages of stumbling emptiness,
pinned with wooden pins weathered
into slight perching birds.
We watched the wind whipping the sheets,
and Mother staggering down the row, up and down.

Afternoons she brought frozen white sheets
one at a time from the line. A trick, sleight-of-hand,
how in her downstairs bedroom
they finished drying like snow drifting on the bed,
how she carried them stiffened like poster board,
how she fitted them until they looked
like a soft white bandages. She did this so I could say:

Here are the sheets that rose up to us.
Here is the way we put our arms around them.
Here are the patterned quilts.
Here is the coverlet loomed by her grandmother.
Here are the horizon-clean sheets on all our beds.
Here is the room its glow of fatigue deceived by lamplight.
Here are our lives blown free.

My Father's Cows

The tame ones nudge him for treats.
If the grass gets too short,
he moves them to new pastures.
When the cattle buyers advise
to thin-out the older ones, he refuses.
They won't go to a slaughterhouse.
Whistling them in for their safety,
the cows come with young calves in tow.
He's worried about the deep digging
along the fencerows
maybe fox or coyote dens.
Evenings, until he calls them
they graze on a slice of a distant hillside.

The Journeys

> *(They) . . . pressed round to embrace him,*
> *kissing him on his head and shoulders and*
> *taking hold of his hand.*
> —*The Odyssey*, Book XXIV

1.
Like Odysseus my father wanders
past hungry pigs, spotted Poland Chinas
in a bare lot nosing out shelled corn,
the breed his father nurtured.

2.
My father in the field when we awakened—
out of school and underfoot, summer flotsam.
He was still there after we were sound asleep.
One year, our shadow father said,
"Never again," the taxes taking half of his crops.
Sundays, we ate together at the dining table,
round as a globe I saw in a geography book—
platters placed like continents,
North America, Australia, Asia—
fried chicken, mashed potatoes, gravy.

3.
One steamy afternoon, he gets lost
in someone else fields, his heart beating fast,
and my mother's hospitalized.
When we find him, we rubbed his chapped face.
Scarcely able to walk, he swore the road was changed.

4.
New Year's Eve, the crowd in Times Square's wild.
I keep time with my foot and pull my father
out of the chair, my arms around him.
I take his left hand in mine.
An old sick father and his aging daughter,
two-stepping to big band music, dance in the New Year.
My mother and brother smiling at us.

Fairfax Community Hospital

Suppose the drugs don't help?
The nurse puts a cool cloth
on her head, gives her a sip of water.
She wants her daughter.
We are near her bed,
our hands like sacks of flour.

She's in the kitchen,
rolling out egg noodles
on a white enamel table
for early dinner.
She hears him calling,
Mary, what time is it?

The American Character

My father's cows would walk into the North Sea.
They tromped his listed fields to get sweet clover.
They leaned into fences that didn't hold them.

Here in Cumbria, around English lakes,
Cattle stand in shallow streams, they rub their heads
Against fences made of stones and meditate.

The British have not pulled out their hedgerows,
Replacing them with woven wire fences.
They trim them and stack the limestone,

Their cattle grazing placidly, not like his,
Hanging their heads over barbed gates to eat
Grass exactly like the grass under their feet.

Frank Field's Weather Report

My parents could order flat seeds
bound to give seedless
pink tomatoes or morning glories
opening like a saxophone flare,
the blue bell scored purple.
They didn't have to believe,
only listen intently,
the way young love goes on and on.
Every morning the nearness of his voice
a comfort. He promised
everything: rain, gusts
to thirty-five miles, snow, ice,
temperatures a hundred degrees
or more. He's always been
on the radio. My parents
never disappointed,
not even when cold bullets of hail
bigger than meatballs damaged crops,
our new car under the maple tree,
its shiny blue paint bruised.
Never disappointed,
always turning to tune in—

Memory's Fragment

Her small slippers on the Singer's treadle
at the foot of their bed
until my parents retired and moved to town.
My brother said he could hear Mother
crying at night after he'd go upstairs.
She's brought into the front room,
she was home for a last visit.

Every Saturday Night

My father swore at his cattle, swearing they could open gates,
And at hydraulic lifts with missing bolts bound to be lost.
He raged at glacial rock he believed, with prescience,
Had rolled into fields to dull his plowshares,
Loosen the bolts and dangle the washers
Until a sound like castanets traveled about the wheels.
The ground spread open like chocolate cake.
His one good mare was Maud,
But the other half of the grey-roan team that wouldn't pull, Sonofabitch.
Large-spirited heads, Belgian, they trotted,
Unless the wagon was loaded, smartly together.
It was the darker mare making my father blaspheme
The Lord's name.
I think now those blue strings of epithets
Were his solemn prayers,
The swearing at the lazy mare his Ave Marias
When the world looked its blackest.

My father knew the names of trees
We outlined on thin paper for school,
Labeling the leaves pinnate and lobed.
He watched the thunderheads move
And held an uneasiness about the world.
The year of bumper crops, golden loads hauled from every field,
He drove home a dark blue Impala,
The hubcaps, like tinfoil, and narrow strips
Of chrome from fender to fender.
I thought there was nothing he couldn't do. No one he couldn't save.
In the backseat we all sang—I'm looking over a four-leaf clover
That I overlooked before.
Saturday nights—always late, I ran to the car,
Starched and painted, my lips as red as a rooster's ass, he said.
But I never blotted the lipstick. I pressed my mouth
To set the color like ingénues in old movies.

Jubilant,

wearing new dresses, our mothers
drove to Ladies Aid, folded handkerchiefs
hung from their pockets
like the wilted cucumber vines in our gardens.
On the way home, smears
of Kool-Aid on our clothes
as we balanced over the front seat,
listened to plans
for another meeting. They had pieced quilts,
exchanged cake recipes, new remedies
for poison ivy: *Apply wet soda, wrap with gauze.*
I could never wait for the cure—
So much to do, so much sunlight going by,
Bicarbonate streaking our brown legs.

Grocery Shopping

The Alzheimer's patient himself never knows his memory has been erased, His life is simply missing.
                        —*Newsweek*
                         November 1988

My silent father is dressed in clean overalls,
Riding beside me like a sullen child.
I keep my foot steady at fifty-five driving
the curved highway. It's in my blood—
speeding, pushing the limit, taking control.
He's driven me on impassable roads
to ballgames, captain of the team,
I can't miss a game. He'd shift down,
keep the speed, double-clutch and we'd
catapult over the chug holes.

Now I'm driving with care as he did,
counting his cattle, checking crops.
Today he seems uneasy and drawn,
like in a close game when he played basketball.
I can tell he's lost weight, his hands bony.
His oversized cotton shirt blouses out,
deceiving like big ears of corn empty
in a drought. He doesn't seem strong.
When neighbors question Mother
about his health, she hides her concern, saying
It's his chartreuse colored pickup.

I carry on routine as women must do,
Down one aisle, bread, milk, down the next,
Lunch meat, potatoes, apples, coffee,
Then Ritz crackers. He follows shuffling his feet,
I want him to stand straight. He looks haunted
And sheepish when a friend calls his name.
I drive around while he waits for me.
Why didn't I notice he's growing smaller
Every moment? I don't know if he knows
Who I am, his oldest child, the most difficult,
The one with his face.

His aunt tells how as a child, he deviled his mother
for candy and chewing gum, but she doesn't
mention a word of his running away, eighteen,
wanting wages, money of his own to spend.
My grandfather drove all night to bring him
back home. He'd have the car Saturday evenings,
with pocket money to splurge on my mother.
Hurriedly, I stop, gather the brown grocery sacks,
my father into the car for the ride home.

I drive fast, lifting us groundless as we top the hills.
Letting up on the foot-feed takes our breath
away as when despairing of failed crops,
the odds being we'll win next year, the old grasp
Of planting and harvesting still in our hands.

 Turning in the drive, he sees an empty garage—
"Damn, she's not here." He thinks he's alone.
I put my hand over his, my faith in my mother.
"She's here," I say, "We're in the car."
He pulls away, places his arm on his chest,
as he might have done in grade school,
pledging the allegiance to the American flag.

Wolf School

Raining at recess, I stayed
at my desk to practice penmanship exercises.
At four o'clock, I gathered my books,
going with Richard dizzy from insulin shots.
At the corner, I walked south,
as he struggled on to the top hill.
At the Christmas program, our teacher lined us
up to dance to the Highland fling
wearing Scottish kilts and berets.
The fathers grimaced in the small desks
as our mothers smiled, wearing nice coats,
spotted clean with white kerosene.
Even in his heavy shoes,
Richard's feet flapped like a vaudevillian comic.
I took his hand, stepping forward and back,
bowing and curtsying.
Cars were leaving the driveway one at a time.
We waved out the car windows,
and then at the corner, frantic waving
to each other as if it were the last day of school.

                                              Richard Dunlap
                                              1934-1942

Raising Animals

At the barn door, nodding, docile and attentive,
The lambs watched me.
I carried black-nipple bottles of formula to them,
Their sober faces partitioned my days.
That fall, when ankle-deep grass was sadness
And the days darkened earlier,
My parents said the lambs have to be sold.
They say before cold weather. They say before hard snows.
A winter's sting in my eyes, I fell into bed.
The sheep, silent and apocryphal, stared at me
Until morning came like the realization of sin.

That spring my father steered
The bobbing flock of Hampshire Down ewes toward me,
He looked mythic coming closer and closer
Through ground-clouds, towing two lambs
With impenetrable dreamy neck-wool.
Their underbellies smooth as the inside of a woman's leg.
I touched their noses and looked into their ears.
I held them in my arms all summer,
Learning to negotiate a disappearing world,
Telling myself if it gives nothing
Then it can demand nothing.
It was my father who kept his Angus cows
After they were too old to calve,
My brother feeding abandoned strays that stayed on and on.

Why hadn't I the knowledge to single out
Something preservable? Some people love willow trees.
Why did I ignore my sister, sitting on the well,
Nursing with her fingertips the newest kittens?
I believed careful selection of Old Testament names,
Ones that parents give children,
Would be a name even lambs can grow into.
I was married before I remembered
My mother never gave names to her show bantams,
Bronze-feathered hackles glinting in the light.
Her anonymous hens peered from cartons,
Protecting six small eggs dark as agates.

They had feet like vultures, the hens lacked grace, I'd say,
admiring my lambs trotting after the bottle in step.
What difference were the deep snows?
In daylight, I didn't know the truth.
For weeks, I prayed, please god, my lambs.
In dark nights, they stand two warm, reasonable faces
At arms length when someone I love blames me
For what I can't change.

On Christmas Day, 1989

A mother decries her son's death,
if only he had waited. An Australian girl tells
her mum's a widow at fifty.
The lights of cities flicker in the distance.
Who wouldn't be ecstatic thinking
of seeing a family member in the East
the first time in twenty-seven years.
Our train surges to Berlin.
One husband and wife have brought
a crate of chickens, someone else tethers a goat.
We're all crammed together like soldiers.
My brother has a hammer and chisel
in an L.L. Bean knapsack used
to take a piece of the Wall away.
We hardly notice the cold winter air blowing in.
Can names written on paper scraps
help families find loved ones?
They'll search for marked graves,
to chronicle someone they've lost.
I'll tell friends how packed together we were,
pimpled Americans, ruddy West Germans,
and sweet Belgian women—
all feeling the push forward. I, too,
am watching the lighted German towns.

Yellow Short Haired Tabby

I have given you away.
I wonder if you are safe
from the eagles cruising
the yard of your new mistress.
The red-tailed hawks might take
you in one wide swoop.
They nest on the high-rises along the bayou.
Here you were only safe on my lap.
Looking out the window
to see you climbing the oak tree, I gasped.
Surely you have learned,
from the lady who stole you,
you're a gift, found under the freeway,
a beloved immigrant.

Driver's Ed

If crops were good, my father left
on a winter morning, never telling anyone
his plans to buy a new car, usually
a Chevrolet, black or grey, having
the most comfortable seats.
My brother, only twelve, was allowed,
to drive taking gravel roads to get tractor parts.
In decent weather, he'd hole up
in the new car's back seat
on the soft upholstery reading comic books,
Superman and *Wonder Woman*.
We could play the radio too.
It was like a library for us,
a hideaway from sundry tasks,
like feeding the cats, setting the table.
I decided I needed to be a driver, too.
Under the steering wheel,
I felt for pedals with my foot,
the brake, the clutch.
When I asked how to shift gears,
my brother mumbled, the left one, the clutch.
He didn't look up,
"Push in the brake and clutch,
down for low, up for second, down, high."
With a lurch, the car stumbled forward,
I glanced back, his eyes opened wide
like Bambi in the forest.
The comic book, lying on the plush seats, had
Wonder Woman in scant clothing,
brandishing a silver sword.

You Leave for the Office

Then I hear our dog's shallow breathing,
His heart racked by Cushing's.
He holds his head sideways
Like the perverse woodpeckers
While tattooing holes in our pine tree,
Transplanted from a Texas forest.
The red berets of the Picidae family
Could fly off in the frantic act
Of defacing our indigenous tree.
Their speckled breasts pushed against
The knobby trunk remind me
Of women from Long Island,
Shopping Macy's after-Christmas specials,
Jerking sweaters from my hands.
Using a friend's discount who works
In advertising, I wonder if it were
worth the shoving and elbowing.

When MacDuff and I leave to avoid the heat,
We begin a slow walk toward shade.
He's doing well for being hit by a car
When younger, my fault for allowing
Him to go on a walk with a neighbor.
Unbelievable now, but dogs often took
Themselves on a little stroll.
Now there's no safety for my crossing
The street, let alone a dog or cat,
Perusing the neighborhood.

The Day of the Trucks

Mornings, when trucks came to load
Our livestock for market, the pigs took
Their own sweet time nosing
Shelled corn from the earth,
Their soft pink noses lifted, sniffing the air,
A refusal to walk the plank.
In the truck bed, the cattle lift their heads for air.
Do the ones returned for better prices
Tell of hammers and blood and carcasses?

Summer Journal

The pigs basking, bellies lowered
in cool mud, the milk cows standing
in creek water under overhanging willow trees,
I traipsed through the blue grass
to sit and journal under a large maple,
I described my newest heart throb,
a star forward with blue eyes.
Striding the court, dark curls,
falling in his face, the clock ticking,
it's the last quarter, everyone on their feet.
We have the ball, only ten seconds;
a fast break to the basket, he scores.

Red Gloves

I'm with a nephew and his wife
in Amsterdam, touring the museums,
the Rijksmuseum with Vermeers
and Rembrandts, the Van Gogh
with paintings of flowering orchards,
incandescent faces, mythic landscapes.
Searching for a lost glove to no avail,
then trudging back icy streets
to the Museum, I saw taped high
on the ticket-window glass a glove,
not my ordinary maroon glove,
now a still life glove.
Adjacent to the ticket-lady's glass,
a wall of his irises and cherry trees.

What the Bell Told

Even in our best wedding picture,
my husband's child sticks his hand in,
fingers stiff like a starfish
or firecracker, a flower of his fingers,
springing us partly apart mid-rib.
I am wondering now if a grown child
conceived out of another's hunger
for permanence will stall my breath.
A dated holly bell, silver-plated,
from a friend reminds me
that the sound of childlessness is empty.
It follows me, open and full, comes
back just like that, the pure white air
where I live, where I pray.

Threshing

If the yellow stickers are cut,
I go barefooted, two barrettes
holding back my straight hair.
Virgil Willis pulls his threshing machine
into our wheat field, its tracks
like a Mesozoic creature.
I go with my father to pick up repairs
for the machine from Mike Johnson,
who can fix carburetors, radiators,
a real jack-of-all-trades.
He tells us a black panther is loose
on the Nodaway river bottom—
paw prints the size of a plate,
his hands making a circle, middle fingers
and thumbs, touching on each hand.
Though Missouri heat's unbearable,
I lock my windows, taking
no chances of loose wildcats.
Taking water whenever a load of wheat come in,
I hear the men's sotto voce voices
near quitting time. They refuse to ride
in wagons pulled by tired horses.
My uncle leads the grey mares to water
as the farmhands walk toward the barn.

Determined to Go Fishing

We hurried up the driveway
to our galvanized cattle-tank with found
small sticks, a white cotton string tied
to each stick, a safety pin at the end of each string.
Although children have drowned there,
a cautious child, I've never broken a bone,
or fallen from a tree. Trying hard,
but I never caught a catfish on a safety pin.
My brother did.
Elated, he skipped to the house,
his ugly fish tethered high in the sky.
Do you remember that fish, I asked
talking to him on the phone,
its downward mouth as if it were crying.

When School Is Out

I hardly ever played with dolls,
preferring jumping rope,
giving my brother rides on his new bicycle
he couldn't balance on.
Gathering eggs, we pulled setting hens off the nests.
They looked Elizabethan
waddling away in ruffled feathers.
When a cousin my age came to visit,
we helped in the garden.
Afternoons, we drove toy cars and trucks
in the dusty dirt around the pine's exposed roots
making bridges, a highway, and parking spaces.
My brother had the red convertible
while she wanted the yellow sedan.
I was left with the two-door black car
that had big tires.

Traveling North to Köln

My sister's daughter cups
her hand under her chin,
looking at lighted houses
along the train tracks.
Her face in profile,
she has my sister's bone structure,
her cheeks rising like hills above
the blinking lights of towns.
I can imagine it's pre-world war,
we're on a train carrying
us toward an Italy holiday,
but we are close to where the Americans
pushed through to free Paris,
then fought to the finish in Belgium.
On December 25, 1944 my uncle,
with a tank battalion in Bastogne,
survived. He didn't know
his daughter had been born
early enough in the day to go
under the Christmas tree.
Now near the City of the Dome,
my brother's child asleep,
her face like an angel.

Residing Next Door

My friend is gone, a good friend,
nothing else need I say. He wore
lush fur, meowing how are you, I'll be
your confidant. I've plenty of time,
no dull meeting, no saving accounts
(save my friends), no mickey-mousing around,
only wondrous new days, inky dark nights.

Thoughtful, he toured the neighborhood.
Poirot, you good-natured fellow, speed
onward to newer smells, tastier meals.
I'll look for you under a leaf, beneath the ferns,
in the moon. For your kindness,
for the spirit you brought, I only ask
that someone charitable pet your head.

                              Poirot,
                              1997–2011

Deer Season

                Red leaves tumble,
           dull-blades, like children
righting inside-out socks.
          To rake these peripatetic
                  leaves, impossible—

                Across the street a deer
            drifts from a sycamore,
dendrite antlers, velvet coated,
            eyes open wide.
                    I've never comforted anyone

                in their dying moments.
            Only after clothed in silk,
mannequin-faced, not theirs.
            I remembered
                her smile and the laughter.

                Under winter snows,
                falling leaves hiding seeds. Every spring,
sun and rain push the pink oxalis
            out of the dark earth,
                where we undecided must go.

Squatters

I stop chasing the dog
to check the wren nest
between a mop and old broom,
hiding three speckled eggs,
laid by a tiny female.
Opening like a cave
the nest of spit, sticks and straw,
sleeps three bedraggled,
naked chicks. When served
dinner by devoted parents,
they waited open-mouthed,
looking like a Methodist church choir.
In and out, father and mother flew,
back and forth.
The hatchlings, soon will be wearing
light grey fuzzy sweaters—
Oh no, have they gone
away from the little broom!
My eyes search the rooftop.
They've flown like you, far away.

Burned to the Ground

I looked straight ahead,
past the house-grave,
over the gambrel
roofed barn, weathered gray,
to see the lay
of empty fields, the curves
and turns of earth.
Driving back, the rope swing,
rotted away.
The battered white-pine's
limbs torn by high winds
leave blank pages of sky.
My home's gone underground.

Conversion at the Dome

Nothing is so important to man as his own state,
Nothing so formidable to him as eternity
—Pascal

Thinking existence an endless dream,
I didn't go with others touring the Cathedral
With beautiful stained glass and rows of pillars,
A kind of paradoxical cube. Now I go alone.
The bell tower spirals five hundred nineteen
Sandstone steps, pleated around a center pole.
It's like climbing to God—
A mystical unwinding of the self—
Sculptured angels, teetering on a high ledge,
hold symbols of the Passion—cockerel, hammer, nail.
The bell tower's door conceals an ideal
Like train schedules.
I climb higher and higher, beginning to understand,
Before engines, the devotion of twelve men
Ringing St. Peter's bell.
What I believe in is distance.
Between the cities of God, the workers faithfully work
Adding grey stone to the Dome.
My pupils, my irises are like stained glass.
My eyes are garments of my face,
The madonnas of my body.

The Rule of Participation

You were barely able to pull yourself up
to the crib railing. I'd clamp your hands there
so that you took your first steps at ten months,
hanging onto the wainscoting.

Our parents were busy, going over
grain and seed receipts from a rented farm
where we lived, where I held your hands
and where you stepped away from me.

But if you could rent time as you rent space,
or even better like electric lines,
networked by special right-of-way,
I should be able to put on your disease

like a snowsuit, feel my feet pointed,
stretch it on, with my arms into your arms,
little finger, index finger, ring, middle finger,
and thumb, put on all the hurt,

walk door to door with your pain, scaring dogs
and children. Then we could laugh,
saying it's over like dinner going cold on the table.
Perhaps I planned it that way.

I saved you once. We were playing and you fell,
your front baby teeth jammed
into the roof of your mouth so I reached in,
pulled them out. I want to do it again,

I want us watching from steamed winter-windows,
our mother looking like a Russian soldier,
scattering buckets of shelled corn,
clumps of Rhode Island hens following her.

I want the notched board in the rope swing,
our feet denting the sky, our heads reared,
backs arched, the forty-foot spruce in the other corner,
swinging wide beside the white pine.

Ominous

In the field's northeast corner
a remnant of an old country school,
fenced off,
its broken-down foundation, ominous as a mass grave,
covered in vines and treacherous briars.

My father warned us not to go there after he had seen black snakes
sunning on the soggy ground that spring.

Late one morning, a tree full
of black snakes, born contortionists,
stretched their onyx bodies into slick walking sticks
in our sycamore, sloughing off
onion-peel skins, depositing them in the yard at our feet.

Amazed at their brazen spring rites,
I never again picked wild raspberries near the old school.
Taking my baby sister for walks,
we avoided the cryptic relic, walking over one hill,
no farther, only one hill.

Storyline

Naming the characters in books I'd read,
my grandfather listened intently.
He never flinched as I started to recite
detailed plots, this child, an orphan,
this kind heroine, penniless.
He died in the summer for no good reason.
Painting my nails red, dabbing Blue Waltz
on my wrists, my exacting grandmother
gone in a winter so cold
our breath billowed
white clouds in the air as we said goodbye
under staunch trees with bare branches.

Neighbors said my father's father,
the hardest worker they had ever known.
We admitted his health problems
when he committed suicide. His obituary
laudatory, well-respected, industrious,
much loved by his family and friends.
For all I know, he wanted to call it day
(or a life). My grandmother worried,
his knee pain dire, he was unable to walk.
She may have placed her head against her Singer,
clacking out the irreverent print dresses,
I wore to school, praying he'd get better.

My Husband

It's the rain
when I miss him
most and the knowing what he's reading.
He touches me to listen
to the drops like little hammers
on the tin lawn chairs,
the dog pawing at us to let
him outside only to want
to come back, his muddy feet
walking across our fleece blanket
as we settle down
with our morning coffee
to read away the thunder.

The Lace School

Balstr. 11, 8000 Brugge, Bruges, Belgium

On a street, lined with blossoming trees,
Catholic children take classes,

learning how to make elegant laces.
Following patterns pinned to pillows,

they move the bobbins with sleight of hand,
crossing and twisting,

left over right, right over left, one stitch,
its like reading poems,

one image, one metaphor at a time.
When threads tangle, devoted students work,

uncross and untwist their mistakes.
Readers open their books again.

Surveillance

In the fourth grade we marched,
two at a time, into the empty second grade room.
The County Nurse checked
the skin on our bellies,
boys first, their blue overall suspenders
down around their spindly legs.
Then we girls raised our skirts
so they could slide our panties
down around pelvic bones,
smooth as the rounded end of small, green pears.
We survived it.
They checked the clouded
skin on my slight belly for *itch*,
a prevalent, contagious skin disease.
We knew who had it.
They were bathing in a medicine
smelling like rotten eggs.
Marking positive on a card for me to take home,
I didn't believe her lie.
I knew I didn't have it, although it took
a doctor's note to tell the teacher
I only had dry skin.

Lies

After ten years, happily married,
And watching relatives and friends plan
Their lives together, the young woman hadn't
A notion that a man would ever lie to her,
The person he holds dear; she thought
That courtship was courtly, taken
From the Old French, meaning to act
In a dignified and ceremonious
Manner, that like the good Sir Gawain, a man
Would carry even into the business world
His lady's embroidered and perfumed
Handkerchief (or perhaps just his idea
Of her, the odor of her body), the one whose
Drawn breath, remembered, makes him hard
Going down the wide hall to a white
Sterile bathroom to urinate before
Returning calls, the pink slips lying akimbo
On his mahogany desk, the same way she dropped
Her underwired bra and panties on the red carpet
The first time they made love.

There Are the Lilacs

Elsewhere the street bends formally,
A stiff sunlight curving the corner.

As a child I'd find the monkey wrench gone
From my father toolbox. It floated in the air like down.

Why can't we see aggravation as useful and natural
Like blizzards and heat waves? Then those day-in-day-out sorrows

Could hang around our necks like old woolen scarves.
Once I drove rain from bright maple leaves with a hot iron.

I needed the clear flat love from the world saved,
Pasting four of them on brown paper, hoarding the wine-red color.

To have owned a maple leaf matters, since I don't understand
The charm of authenticity in geography books—

Miles of white beaches marking the upper Pacific coastline,
Cliffs that drop into a turning ocean.

I was too far away to jump into the waves.
Versailles' garishness didn't appall me either,

Only townsfolk shuffling by in sneakers and designer skirts.
But the Hall of Mirrors told me truth—

The sky glozes over the gaudy rooms.
In my country, the wide cumulus clouds seemed like time exploding.

I cup my hands to catch it. There are the fields that fed us
As long as we asked. There are the marigolds, wild millet and wheat.

I'll put my arms around everyone's father who doesn't remember.
I'll tell them I don't know where I am.

It's the only absolute I know. I cling to the white rising mist,
Ride it up a hill like the elephant that came to town.

When we were young, my father talked of driving to the Black Hills,
Across the Badlands where outlaws hid.

Now he says he won't go anyplace.
No one makes decisions for him. He won't hear my mother.

They moved into town, renting the farm,
And in the daytime, he reads about train robbers, bank holdups,

And Indian tribes who lived on the prairie.
He knows how his family found their way from Tennessee.

I say I'm home, but I wake again and again.
How did I get here? Paris is hours ahead.

The electric globes of light glow in my home
And make the living room like a street, luminary and dissociative—

I'll change it back to another time. I see the clean blade
Of the plow reflecting our driveway, not quite dark yet.

It's a spring evening with a haze of lilacs overhead—
Our voices are vigilant and full of particulars.

Planting Trees in A Field My Father Dug Rocks From With His Own Hands

> *I'm in love with what you stood for.*
> *May we be keen stewards of our land, our legacy,*
> *May we sow unconditional love*
> *And be stubborn like Missouri clay—*
>   —Levi Osburn

Though my brother hauls my suitcase
to the cab each time we stop at antique stores,
three in Dearborn off Interstate 29,
then to get a hamburger, the ride is hectic
in his new blue pickup to the farm. We're
replanting the young saplings eaten by deer.
I vaguely remember one spring
following a wet winter, my father didn't have
time to set posts and nail the barbed wire,
separating the planted ground from
the mushy pastures turning a lush green.
A month of melting grey snow and the April rains,
now the corn needed to be planted.
My brother daydreamed while he watched
the dark, statuesque cattle for two weeks,
keeping them away from the tender green haze
of corn shoots barely above the clotted earth.
At night, the herd of Angus, herded
into a fenced lot east of the house,
lowered heads, bunched together, and slept.
"He was a good farmer," my brother said,
as we drove toward the farm. He plowed
after dark and in dismal weather, often
pestered by salesmen who would follow him
into the fields, through the purple thistles.

Before heaving out the buckets, one with flags
and gel, one with two hundred saplings,
my brother swirls the spare roots in gel to keep
the roots moist. Carrying the lighter bucket
windrow to windrow, setting out spindly green ash

and white oaks to meet conservation rules,
I marked the eaten ones with bright orange flags.
spading deep, he winds each taproot
into a black slice of the dank hillside.
After an hour he slows his pace. I think
of my father summer evenings, my skipping
in front of him and then falling behind.
I wanted him to hurry, but he kept the same
steadfast steps, watering the white-faced calves.
Waiting for him, I straddled a wooly lamb,
rubbing its small nose, trying to find
the orifices of its wet breathing when a ram
butted me over a high gate. Landing on boards
with rusty nails, I cried loud tears.
My knees cut and bleeding, no one came
so I limped to the house for mercurochrome.
After supper, like a tick I hung around
as the adults played pitch, a garrulous, little ghost
at their card table. Counting their cards,
I would screw up my face at bad hands,
talk in non-stop spiels.

At the first airport entrance, my brother pivots
next to the glass door of Southwest gates.
I get my suitcase in hand and wave to him.
sitting alone, I offer to take a snapshot of a family.
For absolutely no reason, the loud speaker spews
my name like I'm there again, a daughter,
botherer, magpie, jumping to rapt attention.

> For Don, 11-2-1936
> October 23, 2016

Eye Lashes That Blinked You Love Me

My little dog is a heartbeat at my feet.
          –Edith Wharton

Everything was out of whack today.
the scotch tape's in the oven,
my head for thinking, now only for mourning.
I could break all my clocks like Auden did.
I'd rather cut all fences, letting animals,
far and wide feel the wind in their long ears,
like Cecil, hanging his head out the car window,
showing an underbite every bit as charming
as the Wife of Bath's gap.
Cecil arrived to live here, eating a shoe, only one.
Sway-back, splay-footed, and zebra-striped legged—
A sprinter and a parachuter—
Eyelashes unrivaled.
My orders to stop at a street corner weren't heeded.
He crossed the street into a park,
disappearing into bamboo hedge.
I drove around the block three times,
down an alley and back to the park, up the Boulevard
and back, frantic. I found him
sitting on his short little haunches, proud of his escape—
My heart still beats faster, thinking of him lost.

Gypsy Territory

The gypsies should have gotten me,
wrapped me in sheets the way
they snapped silverware from cabinets.
After sleeving a stewing rooster.
they would move through the countryside
in red convertibles, parking stretched
along the shoulder like exotic garter snakes,
the kind an aunt of mine caught,
laying on a step to tease her brothers.

Then the men told how the gypsies stole piglets,
anything loose, and children.
They counted the times in the last five years
something had disappeared,
a scythe, a shovel, and once a young mule,
loaded into a trailer and driven away.
I would have gone with that mule.
She never laid a tooth on me even though
they said mules bite like hell.
She nuzzled me when I brought her sweet corn.

Away at school I had my own books and a desk
but I must have been over twenty
before I had reason to go west of Kansas.
I'm like a water witch's hazel-stick
pulled down by some underground river—
I still want to go back.
Now when I'm alone and this isn't the life I meant,
I wish they'd stolen me.
I would have ridden the rumble seat,
never turned my head, never said home once.
I wish love were as sure and real as weather.

The Autumn Moon

        This is pretty and fitting for you,
Written on a gleaming postcard
            You sent to me
        From where you're studying
The philosophy of law.
         Light is falling across Oxford.
              Above the steep black roofs,
Red sun or new moon, it's impossible
        To tell on the card.

        An azure haze hovers over
The spires and dark buildings,
            Romantic and distant.
        Months later, in Houston, driving
The freeway to work
        Past Transco Tower, I saw
            A pale circle searching for
Darkness in the tall pine trees
        And blue morning.

        It looked like child's play,
Pasted, exact and strange in the light,
            But it's wasn't play at all—
        It's a real morning,
Your death in my throat six months,
           I watched teenagers on Banks Street
              Wasting their lives
Like fire burning up stars that fall
        To earth.

        When I passed them,
One boy flipped his white ass, bare,
            An astrological object out of place.
        Jerking up his pants,
They all scuttled away, going to class,
           Snorting, heads high,
              A single team.
Why don't they
        Understand nakedness?

      If anything's worth thinking,
It's worth thinking all the way,
              Mother, lover, sister, wife, whore—
    Our grief part of us
In the beginning.
      I remembered
           Going to school
In a made-over red paneled truck
      Seats placed lengthwise.

      Harley Woods, a nasty
Freckled-faced boy shoved me under
           The driver's curved seat,
    Saying terrible words,
Dirty, nasty, mean words.
      I wanted him thrown off the bus
           But the driver squinted,
Keeping his eyes on the road,
      Never once looking around.

Black and White Snapshot

I'm looking at a photo,
My sister, brother, and me.
I'm the oldest, hair neatly combed,
Hands on my knees.
We're sitting on steps, a screen door
Behind us with Victorian wooden brackets,
My sister one year old, my brother, seven.
He has the sweetest smile,
His arm wrapped adoringly around her.
Why couldn't we have stayed,
Loving our parents, no obligations,
His sweet smile in perpetuity.

Visiting the Dickinson Homestead

At Amherst College Library, I held a reddish lock
of Emily Dickinson's hair in my hand,

the color the same as her hallway portrait
where her dark hair pulled back tight into a kind of expediency.

Inside a small drawer in her bedroom, I saw
her neatly scripted notes, written on scraps of paper,

a private fascination with the world, lost love, and death.
Her precise silhouette on the bedroom wall

reminded me of the cutting of my Scottie dog,
Pulling the leash with determination.

Ms. Dickinson's speared words, one by one, one poem,
then another, intent that every day would be

a fiery ritual: bud and bloom: emotion.
She tied the poems together with ribbons to save in black and white

her thoughts of the uncertainty of life.
I, too, would like a room so sparse, what matters, matters—

her upstairs window had sweeping views of tall trees,
green pastures of yellow and pink flowers in Spring.

In Autumn, roiling leaves, golden and scarlet.
I watched someone racing a chestnut mare on a path.

Her side garden, down eight stone steps, stealthy, constant,
secluded, growing roses, daffodils, crocus, clumps of trillium,

then climbers and floribundas flashing in the summer
beside pear and cherry trees and rows of yellow and cream daylilies.

Her white daisies say nothing. "Forgive my forgetting,"
she tells her inaccurate minister,

"Understanding grows slowly like landscape."
Whether it's love or the last word I want is no clearer

than handwritten lines penned at her desk,
the exacting metaphors squirming into the margins.

Suffolk Ewes

Late into the evening light,
I want the earth or nothing—
Their half-black painted faces angle
Like smudged quotation marks around an indigenous exactness,
The contour of ground, the run of the field.
Alone at night, they sleep,
Soft pallets under hedgerows,
Hoarding the white heather with its good fortune,
Remembering the banks and banks of wild rhododendron.
No matter what's retrievable, they should dream
Of native wildflowers.
As if directives, they teeter, white-woolly and top-heavy.
On truest hillsides, they preserve by contrast
The color-swell of bluebells.
They are elegant in the tinged light.
Mid-morning, their open-throated lowing—
The hyphenated vowels—is out of earshot.
How is it they speak in their silences?
I see them nod and believe every word.

Catbirds

I Migrations

I've often seen the killdeer on her grounded nest.
In pastures, she fluttered, fearful
under the rush and noise of my father's machines.
I know her circus performance, limping away
in a primitive gait, a ruse to save her young.

My parent's migration last year from farm to acreage,
from stove to silver radiators—
the kind that warmed the sixth grade—
has changed their perspective to a yard,
a clearing, and a row of apple trees
aggravated by sounds of catbirds in the sunlight,
mewing like a cloud of hungry kittens.

Now the catbirds in a small elm tree tease,
sky-fish in my window view.
A few days ago they interlaced like acrobats
crossing, turning, touching each other.
Their empty nest eyes me, a grown daughter,
come to visit and I search the area,
a beacon light, back and forth,
back and forth, for the too-high squalling.

II Pencil Lead, Apples and Snow

Barely the color of pencil lead, the young catbirds
turned into passages from books I can't remember.
The shame of the lost lines was not knowing
they could be found in every book I opened.
I'm sad with the time of brilliant apples,
falling from trees.
Fall reminds me of the ripened-red gloves,
soggy on school radiators,
simmering and waiting for late afternoon.
In the sixth grade, a rancid smell like singed feathers
pinched my nose mid-morning,
grafted Edison's electricity lesson, multiplication tables,
and the flag's pledge to the difficult words I stumbled over.

The seamy odor stripped us of dreams,
we carried home in geography lessons.
Perhaps it was truly alien air,
a treelessness of leaves.
At recess we girls hung upside down, summer birds
on rods, mid-western cranes out of water, awkward and silly.
By four o'clock the scorch-smell made
it seem like I was slipping each hand into the lifeless wing
of a red-apple-colored bird
that had lost its instinctive course.
Afraid, I tightened my fists deep in my mackinaw pockets,
and tried to hug the books close to my heart.
In the evening, the drifting snow sifted-in through the cracks
and sealed my bedroom windows.

III   White Winter, Bright Spring

On dark winters,
the snow sifted down light and weightless
as though soft breast feathers of young catbirds
had filled our road, bank to bank, keeping us home.
Next morning, when my mother threw bread crumbs
into a thick grey yard, the feathers had gone.

Come spring, she watched for the catbirds' nesting to begin,
listened for their calls.
I knew my father sensed an absolute
in the half-grown raccoons he protected at the barn.
About the weather, about the natural forces,
they were mostly of the same opinion,
but she insisted these would kill her chickens.
Holding the burlap shut with his bony hands,
he carried the five cubs to an open field
to turn loose in a hopeful spring
over her protests: "They will come back."

IV Watching Birds

The catbirds will someday fool both my parents,
They will nest unnoticed in the lilac bush.
In my living room, my father holds a robin
like a lump of coal shining into his face.
High noon it flew into the plate glass.
With the bird in his deep-cupped hands,
he wonders why he failed to comfort my mother
about some mutual sadness.

He has waited sixty years for this moment,
to touch the russet color close up
and it was an accident.
Unable to say what we want to hear,
he gives the robin to me
as if its presence were enough.
In dark blue mornings,
my parents' private and reassuring voices
came up through the register.
Whether they are wiser or if they only seem that way,
there's no telling.
They sit on the front porch
and out of sight the catbirds watch.
Together they have picked the wildness out of blackberries
growing in grassy ditches.
Their reflections in the evening light have a silver-blue tinge—
color of water, color of painted radiators,
color of glossy catbirds moving in air.

Thank You

Thanks to my niece Holly Barnes, my best reader, also to my nieces Lynn Kahla and Lori Coulter, nephews Mike Osburn, Mitch Osburn, and Jason Combs, always supportive.

A special thanks to Connor Osburn, my grand nephew, for making visits to his grandparents when they needed someone the most, and for reading my new poems with care.

Thanks to Matt Mayland, a nephew who gave me technical support with much generosity and kindness, and to my friend, Debbie Miller. Thanks to my poet friend forever, Phyllis Koestenbaum; and in memory of my best friend Norma Schneider.

In appreciation of my workshop instructors:

Marie Ponsot, Thomas Lux, William Matthews, Stanley Plumly, Edward Hirsch, Deborah Digges, Jane Shore, Donald Justice, Susan Wood, Adam Zagajewski, Sandra McPherson, Robert Hass, Philip Levine, Cynthia McDonald, David Wojahn, Richard Howard, Sharon Olds, Dave Smith, Dinah Cox.

My workshop classmates, Lisa Lewis, Susan Prospere, Jeff Greene, Michelle Boisseau, Bill Olsen, Nancy Eimers, Rich Lyons, Elizabeth McBride.

A portion of the proceeds from this book will be donated to the Burr Oak Church Cemetery.

About the Poet

Joyce Osburn James grew up in Atchison and Nodaway Counties in Missouri.

She received a B.S. in Education with a major in English and American Literature, and an M.A. in Literature and Literary Criticism from Northwest Missouri State University. She attended the writing program at University of Houston, earning her MFA with honors.

Ms. James has taught creative writing at the University of Houston, Rice University Continuing Education Studies, and Houston Community College.

Joyce James lives and writes in Houston, Texas.

Honors

National Endownment for the Arts fellowship in poetry, 1993-94

Academy of American Poets Prize, University of Houston, 1986

William R. Raney fellowship at Bread Loaf Writers in Vermont, l986

Bediecek Grant to Squaw Valley Writers

First place in the Orange Show Competition, the Brazos Award, and the Houston Festival Award.

Joyce James was also a finalist in:
The Pen Southwest Discovery Prize,
National Poetry Series,
Carnegie-Mellow Series,
Cleveland State Poetry Series,
Brittingham Prize, and others.

She was selected to read at the Conference of College Teachers of English 1992, the M.L.A. Southern Conference and Museum of Fine Arts in Houston, as well as numerous other readings.

Ms. James was nominated twice for a Pushcart prize.

www.ingramcontent.com/pod-product-compliance
Lightning Source LLC
Chambersburg PA
CBHW020949090426
42736CB00010B/1327